T0012378

Candle Magic

Written by
Mikaila Adriance

Illustrated by
Marianna Gefen

PHILADELPHIA

RP Minis®
Hachette Book Group
1290 Avenue of the Americas, New York, NY 10104
www.runningpress.com
@Running_Press

Printed in China

First Edition: August 2023

Published by RP Minis, an imprint of Perseus Books, LLC, a
subsidiary of Hachette Book Group, Inc. The RP Minis name and
logo is a registered trademark of the Hachette Book Group.

The publisher is not responsible for websites (or their content) that
are not owned by the publisher.

Text by Mikaila Adriance

Library of Congress Control Number: 2022951876

ISBN: 978-0-7624-8373-0

LREX

10 9 8 7 6 5 4 3 2 1

Contents

This book has been bound using handcraft methods and Smyth-sewn to ensure durability.

The interior and dust jacket were illustrated by Marianna Gefen and designed by Mary Boyer.

Candle Magic

Written by
Mikaila Adriance

Illustrated by
Marianna Gefen

RP MINIS

PHILADELPHIA

RP Minis®
Hachette Book Group
1290 Avenue of the Americas, New York, NY 10104
www.runningpress.com
@Running_Press

Printed in China

First Edition: August 2023

Published by RP Minis, an imprint of Perseus Books, LLC, a
subsidiary of Hachette Book Group, Inc. The RP Minis name and
logo is a registered trademark of the Hachette Book Group.

The publisher is not responsible for websites (or their content) that
are not owned by the publisher.

Text by Mikaila Adriance

Library of Congress Control Number: 2022951876

ISBN: 978-0-7624-8373-0

LREX

10 9 8 7 6 5 4 3 2 1

Candle Magic: A Quick Overview

Candle magic is a potent form of spellcasting that's endured for centuries in various forms. Think of candles lit outside or inside a church, or, in ancient days, of offerings of incense and other valuables lit aflame as a gift to the gods. You've probably already engaged in some

basic candle magic yourself
if you've made a wish on a
birthday cake.

At its most basic, candle
magic requires just three
things: a candle, something

to light it with, and a specific intention. As long as you have these, you'll be able to perform any type of spell or manifestation; however, if you want to get more in-depth and technical, there are a variety of other tools at your disposal: oils to dress the candle with, incense, sigils, and crystals, to name a few.

Think of the flame as a symbol for the sun: It represents pure will, raw energy ready to be channeled into your desired outcome. We refer to this desired outcome as your *intention*—it's whatever you want to

happen because of your spell.
Everyone's spiritual practice
is different, but generally
speaking, it's good to start by
carefully envisioning what
you want before you ask
the universe for it. If you're
asking for love, for instance,
meditate on what you'll feel
like once you've found your
partner, what type of qualities

they'll have, and what they'll
bring out in you. Imagine
falling asleep next to them
and waking up beside them.
If you want to summon career
success, imagine exactly what
you want: Creative freedom?
Respect? Financial freedom?
A huge salary? Whatever
you want is fair game, and
you should have no qualms

about asking for it—unless it's intentionally harmful to someone else, in which case you might want to reconsider, lest the negative energy comes back to you. (If there's a specific, malicious person in your life you want to deal with using candle magic, there are ways to handle them without doing direct

harm: See "Binding Spell"
for more.)

Once you've visualized
your desire, put your intention into specific, clear
terms. Some witches think
manifestation works best
if you phrase your wish as
though it's already come
true—*I'm so happy with my
supportive partner who makes*

*me laugh every day and appre-
ciates me wholly; I feel valued
and empowered at my new
writing job, and the work I do
is rewarding and high-paying;*
etc.—but the exact verbiage
is up to what resonates with
you. Once your candle is pre-
pared, you will light the flame
while focusing intently on
this thought.

An important note:

It's inadvisable to leave the candle burning when you're not at home, as it's an obvious fire hazard. If you leave before the candle burns fully down, **do not blow it out.** That's spiritually equivalent to snuffing out your wish! Instead, put it out with your fingers or a candle snuffer.

The following sections will introduce everything you can do to "upgrade" your candle. Again, any spell with a candle, a light, and an intention will be powerful enough on its own! But you can enhance the intention by customizing the candle color, by carving it with runes or symbols, by anointing it with oils, by

burning incense beside it, and
by placing it near crystals that
channel the same energy you
wish to harness.

Candle Magic Toolkit

NOTES ON
MAKING AN ALTAR

W hen casting candle
magic, the loca-
tion in which you burn the

candle is very important. Pick somewhere that reso- nates with you within your home—somewhere that feels spiritually safe and beautiful, maybe somewhere that has a personal significance or is near where you spend most of your time.

It will benefit you on your candle-magic journey if you

make an altar. This might
sound intense, but "altar" is
really just a neat shorthand
for what I expressed earlier.
An altar is a sacred space, but
what feels sacred varies from
person to person. It doesn't
even have to be explicitly
religious or spiritual—I
like to think of your altar
as a collection of items that

bring you joy and peace, all gathered in one place. You probably already have all the ingredients for one in your home: photos of loved ones or people you admire, trinkets you've picked up from your travels, and other items with special sentimental value.

This is where you'll want to burn your candle. If you want

to get a bit more witchy, you might consider putting down an altar cloth—a piece of fabric to serve as decoration and confer respect—and adding some crystals and flowers. You can also display images and figures related to your intention, sort of like a vision board, if that's something you're into!

WHAT TYPE OF
CANDLE TO GET?

◆—————✳—————◆

Any candle will work for candle magic. As long as it lights and burns down, it will help you set an intention! However, it's common to use something called a "Seven-Day Pull-Out Candle" when making spells. You can order these online or buy them at a botanica; you can choose the color, which is very helpful, and it's also broad enough to carve symbols and sigils on. But, again, any candle will do. What matters most is the energy you bring.

GUIDE TO
CANDLE COLORS

✳

This is perhaps the simplest way to customize your candle spell: by choosing a specific color. (If you can't find a candle in the color you want, you can cover your candle in glitter or write on it with marker, or even surround it with appropriately colored objects.) Different colors are believed to possess different magical qualities and to attract specific energies, so choosing a

candle of a specific color
can magnify or reinforce
your intention.

On the pages that follow,
you'll find, the most commonly
used candle colors and what
energy each helps to attract.

White

✦ ❄ ✦

Purification, pe**a**ce,
cleansing, new beg**in**nings

Black

✦

Protection, banishing,
releasing negative energy
and bad habits

Red

* ✳ *

Passion, lust, desire, sex,
energy, vitality, courage

Pink

✦ ✸ ✦

Romance, tender love,
self-love, friendship

Yellow

+ ✳ +

Intelligence, mental
clarity, focus, joy,

Green

✦ ☀ ✦

Abundance, growth,
prosperity, fertility,
success, money

Blue

* ✳ *

Healing, inspiration,
truth, renewal,
emotional wisdom

Purple

✦ ✳ ✦

Wisdom, spirituality,
intuition, divination

Orange

✦ ☀ ✦

Creativity, ambition,
career success, confidence,
broadening horizons

Brown

* ✦ *

Balance, stability,
family life

Silver

+ ✴ +

Psychic development,
the moon, divine
feminine energy

Gold

+ ✦ +

Luck, prosperity, power

Additionally, certain days of the week are said to be optimal for lighting certain candle colors. Some colors can work well on multiple days, depending on what your specific intention for them is:

Sunday

yellow and gold

Sunday is (obviously)
the day associated
with the sun, so sunny,
energetic, invigorating
colors are best lit then!

Monday

white, blue, and silver
Perhaps less obviously,
Monday is the day of
the moon, so these
colors, which evoke
the moon's light and
her gentle, mysterious,
emotional energy, work
particularly well then.

Tuesday

red

Tuesday was originally named for Tiu, the Germanic god of the sky and war. In Roman times, it was known as Mars day—another fiery war god. That's why this passionate, intense color is best lit then.

Wednesday

yellow and orange

In Roman times,
Wednesday was Mercury's
day. He's known as the god
of communication, travel,
poetry, and eloquence,
making this an ideal time
to light candles associated
with intelligence, ambition,
joy, and personal growth.

Thursday

purple and blue

Thursday is Thor's day
and, in ancient Rome,
Jupiter's day. Both are the
heads of their respective
pantheons, making
Thursday a perfect day
for candle spells related
to wisdom, spirituality,
truth, and renewal.

Friday

green, pink, brown

Friday was long ago
associated with Venus,
the goddess of love,
fertility, and beauty. If
you're looking to summon
romance, abundance,
material satisfaction, or
desirability, Friday's a
wonderful day to do it.

Saturday

black and purple

Saturday is Saturn's
day; Saturn's energy
is responsible, wise,
authoritative, and a bit
intimidating. This is a great
time to do a protection
or banishment spell, or a
spell that helps with mental
or spiritual growth.

MFRT

GUIDE TO SIGILS

S igils are magical symbols
we create and imbue
with intent to influence the
world around us. Sigil magic

has existed for hundreds of years—there are many complex and nuanced sigils that have been around for centuries, which you can access by simply googling "list of sigils." (The most famous of these is probably the pentagram.)

But that's all a little advanced and intense for our purposes, I feel. It's possible to make your own sigil as well! This is a tool employed by many witches, and it's easy and fun to do. To start, write out an intention. It can be as vague or specific as you want; with sigil magic, shorter is probably better.

Next, cross out all the vowels and repeated letters. Let's say, for instance, your intent is: **I AM SUCCESSFUL AND RADIANT.** With vowels and repeated letters gone, you're left with M F R T.

Then, take the remaining letters and arrange them into an interconnected, geometric design. Feel free to rotate them, resize them, or make them basically unrecogniz-able as letters. When you're done, you'll have your own personal sigil for spellcraft use.

You can take this and incorporate it into your candle however you please. If your candle is broad enough, you might want to carve your sigil into the side of it. Or you might want to draw it on using a permanent marker—or you can simply use your lit candle to burn a small piece of paper with the sigil on it (carefully, over a plate or a bowl of water). As fire consumes your intention, it will release it into the air, sending your energy skyward.

GUIDE TO INCENSES

A nother great tool at your disposal: incense. This is relatively inexpensive and easy to purchase—if

there are no stores near
you selling it, it's abundant
in online stores. Not only
does incense help to center
you, increase your focus,
and bring beauty into your
personal space, but certain
types of incense are believed
to have specific spiritual
properties, which can be

used to reinforce and amplify your intention.

Below, a list of the most common incenses and their uses:

Dragon's Blood

Strength, courage,
potency, chasing out
negative energy, extra
power for any ritual

Frankincense

Purification, good fortune

Jasmine
Love-drawing,
sensuality, relaxation,
mood-enhancement

Lavender

Healing, de-stressing,
sleeping well

Myrrh
Often paired with
frankincense, healing
and meditation aid

Nag Champa
Purification, clearing
of negative energy,
meditation aid

Patchouli

Prosperity, abundance,
fertility, love and lust,
sensuality

Rose
Love, beauty,
devotion, healing

Sandalwood
Tranquility, peace,
banishing negative
energy

Bringing incense into your candle-magic practice is simple: When you light your candle, light your incense as well. Watch both of them release smoke skyward, and visualize your intention floating up alongside it.

GUIDE TO OILS

✦

You can also anoint
your candle in oil to
enhance its effect. Anointing
is easy: Just put a dollop of oil

in your palm, and rub it all over the candle before you burn it.

In terms of choosing an oil, as always, basically anything goes. You're probably best off starting with an essential oil, as they're relatively inexpensive and readily available—or you can even use oils that you have lying around the house, like coconut oil or grapeseed oil.

Below, some of the most
common essential oils and
their properties:

Avocado
Love, beauty, sensuality

Bergamot

Enhancing joy and
strength, clearing
the mind, attracting
good fortune

Cedarwood

Healing, confidence,
rejuvenation, soothing
anxiety

Chamomile
Prosperity, happiness,
relaxation

Coconut
Purification, protection

Eucalyptus
Healing, mental clarity,
protection

Grapeseed
Mental clarity,
prosperity, fertility

Lavender
Healing, relaxation, good
dreams and deep sleep

Olive

Healing, protection,
abundance, love—
sometimes considered
an "all-purpose oil"

Peppermint

Healing, purification,
mental and spiritual
enhancement

Rosemary
Protection, purification,
loyalty, love

Tea Tree
Cleansing, mood
enhancement, removing
blocked energy

Feel free to experiment and combine different oils. You don't have to anoint the candle every time you light it; think of it as a dressing for the first time you burn it.

GUIDE TO CRYSTALS

* ✦ *

Crystals, too, will amplify your candle's power; just place one (or several) nearby for the duration of the burn. As with everything else in spellcraft work, different crystals are believed to have different properties. There are countless different types out there, but here are a few of the most common and powerful, along with their spiritual uses:

Amethyst

+ ✦ +

Calming and tranquility,
psychic protection,
dispelling negative
energy, balance

Aquamarine

+ ✳ +

Calming, soothing,
cleansing, healing,
courage, breaking
bad habits

Black Tourmaline

+ ✦ +

Protection, cleansing,
grounding, banishing
bad energy

Citrine

+ ✳ +

Good luck, joy, confidence,
abundance, creativity

Clear Quartz

+ ✴ +

Healing, cleansing,
energy amplification,
mental clarity

Jade

+ ✳ +

Purity, tranquility, love,
courage, prosperity

Lapis Lazuli

+ ✳ +

Self-awareness,
openness, intellect,
self-expression

Obsidian

+ ✦ +

Shielding against
negativity and psychic
attacks, cleansing,
grounding, protection

Rose Quartz

+ ✳ +

Love, romance, self-love,
sensuality, emotional
healing, heart-opening

Selenite

✦ ✹ ✦

Peace and calm, clarity,
removing blocks,
purification, charging
other crystals

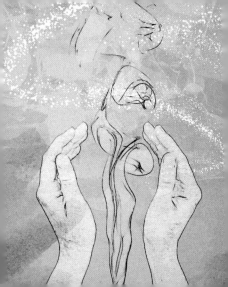

Spells

Now that we have the basics down, we're ready to begin the actual spellwork. These are all rituals based on my own experience; again, if you don't have all the proper ingredients, you can always modify and improvise. And feel free to incorporate other elements

into these spells; for instance,
you might want to draw or
carve a sigil onto the candle
before you anoint it.

LOVE-DRAWING SPELL

This is a means of sum-
moning a new love into
your life; it's not meant to be

used on a specific person but rather to attract *romantic energy* in general. Think of it as supercharging your life with a lovely, alluring, abundant sparkle that will open your heart up and draw the right person in. Perhaps it will be someone you've had your eye on or someone totally surprising!

What you'll need:

+ A pink candle
* Roses (preferably pink or red)
* A bowl of water
+ Honey
* A letter of intention

1. Start by carving a simple sigil on the top of the candle: a heart with your name inside.

2. Anoint the candle with the oil of your choice—I recommend bergamot, olive, or rosemary oil—and run it through incense smoke to purify it.

3. Next, write your letter of intention. Reflect deeply on the traits you want in a partner. These can be

physical or intellectual, abstract or concrete, mundane or strange. Write them in the third person, as if you're describing a person you already know. For instance: *His eyes crinkle when he smiles. She is immensely kind. They always listen intently to my problems with care and consideration.*

4. Put a drop of honey on your fingertip and taste it. Then put another drop of honey on top of the candle, right in the middle of the heart you've carved; this is an offering to whatever deity you're invoking or perhaps to the universe itself. Whichever you prefer!

5. Place the bowl of water in front of the candle.

6. Light the candle.

7. Focus on the flame; watch its reflection in the water bowl. Once you feel centered and ready to go, start to read from your list of desired traits. With each trait you read, pluck a petal

from the rose and let it fall
into the bowl.

8. Once you've finished,
   arrange the remaining
   petals around the candle
   and the water bowl in a
   heart shape.

9. Recite this incantation:

Let the abundant
universe bring my
dream person to me.

As they bring me joy
and fulfillment, so I
shall bring joy and
fulfillment to them.

I open my heart to
love and possibility.
So mote it be.

Suggested Enhancements

Rose or jasmine incense

Bergamot, olive, or rosemary oil *to anoint the candle*

Citrine, jade, or rose quartz

ALLURE-INCREASING
SPELL

✦ ─────── ✦※✦ ─────── ✦

Think of this as weaving
an enchanting web
around yourself; it will make

you appear endlessly compelling and fascinating to others, a mystery they'd love to solve. Although this could definitely help you find love, it's more likely to net you an array of exciting suitors—expect tons of people to start approaching you out of the blue.

What you'll need:

+ A red candle
* Honey
* Red wine
+ A letter of intention, written in red ink
* Sugar and cinnamon mixed together
* A bowl

1. First, write your letter of intention in red ink. This should be as candid as

possible—you're going to
burn it later, so don't worry
about anyone reading it!
Describe your deepest
desires; list the romantic
experiences you've been
craving but haven't let
yourself verbalize—the
things about yourself you
wish someone would intuit
without you having to
say anything.

2. Fold the letter as many times as you can, then sprinkle the cinnamon and sugar on top.

3. Anoint the candle in olive, avocado, or rosemary oil, if it's available, and cleanse it with incense by passing it through the smoke—I'd recommend

dragon's blood, jasmine, or patchouli.

4. Put a drop of honey on your finger to taste it, and then put a drop of honey on top of the candle.

5. Fill a glass of red wine—or a red-tinted fruit juice, if wine isn't an option—and set it in front of the candle as another offering.

6. Light the candle. Once it's burning strongly, use it to set your letter of intention aflame.

7. You should drop your letter of intention into the bowl once the flame gets too large to hold comfortably; if it goes out, you can always relight it (this isn't part of the spell,

necessarily, just a way of protecting your fingers from getting burnt!).

8. As it burns, say the following incantation:

I am an object of fascination, wreathed in mystery and allure.

My heart is a garden behind a palace gate.

Wherever I go, the eyes of all those I want follow along.

With this power, I call forth a dazzling new adventure in love. So mote it be.

Suggested Enhancements

Dragon's blood, jasmine, or patchouli incense

Olive, avocado, or rosemary oil *to anoint the candle*

Obsidian or selenite

MONEY-DRAWING
SPELL

❖————— ✳ —————❖

As the name implies,
this is a very

straightforward spell to help
you manifest money.

What you'll need:

+ A green candle
* A small jar
* Sunflower or olive oil
+ Thyme and basil
* A pen and a piece of paper
* A dollar bill
+ Four coins

1. Begin by preparing your spell jar. Fill it halfway with the oil, then add several leaves of thyme and basil.

2. Next, write the specific sum of money you want on a piece of paper. Fold it in half and place it in the jar.

3. Add the dollar bill as an offering. Screw the lid of the jar on tightly.

4. Anoint the candle in bergamot or chamomile oil, if it's available, and cleanse it by passing it through incense smoke. (Dragon's blood and frankincense are ideal.)

5. Set the candle atop the jar, and surround it with four coins, each set in a cardinal direction.

6. Light the candle, and say
the following incantation:

*I open my arms to
the abundance of
the universe.*

*I accept, without
reservation, the gifts
that are offered to me.*

*Good fortune flows in
ceaselessly, like waves*

breaking on a beach.
So mote it be.

7. When the candle has
   fully burnt down, you can
   dispose of the spell jar
   however you please.

Suggested Enhancements

Dragon's blood or
frankincense incense

Bergamot or chamomile oil
to anoint the candle

Citrine or clear quartz

BINDING SPELL—TO
PREVENT SOMEONE
FROM DOING HARM

❖ ✦ ❖

This is a spell to use
on someone who is

behaving maliciously toward you (or others) and causing harm. It doesn't cause active harm to them—rather, it prevents them from engaging in behavior that hurts others or themselves. Think of it as a metaphysical restraint.

What you'll need:

+ A black candle
* A pen and paper
* A piece of twine
+ Essential oil of your choice
* Incense of your choice

1. Start by preparing your
   candle: Anoint it with coconut,
   eucalyptus, olive, or rosemary
   oil, and purify it by passing it
   through the smoke of dragon's

blood or sandalwood incense.

2. Write the name of the person you wish to bind in the center of your piece of paper. Next, draw a pentagram over it, crossing through the name.

3. Fold the paper in half and bind it with the twine.

4. Press it to your head and repeat the following incantation three times:

With this spell, I bind
you from doing harm.

I bind you from doing
harm unto others, and
I bind you from doing
harm unto yourself.

May you be freed from
your destructive behavior
and find peace.

5. When you've finished
repeating, close with:

So mote it be.

6. Place the paper under your black candle and light it. As the candle burns down, the wax will harden, effectively trapping the target of your spell.

7. Once the candle is fully burnt down, dispose of the remnants and the paper however you please.

Suggested
Enhancements

Dragon's blood or
sandalwood incense

Coconut, eucalyptus,
olive, or rosemary oil
to anoint the candle

Citrine or clear quartz

UNBINDING SPELL— TO LET GO OF A RELATIONSHIP

* ✳ *

This is a spell to sever psychic ties between

yourself and another, freeing
you both from the karmic
shackles of a past relation-
ship. It's a means of fully
letting go so that you can
both move in new directions.

With this type of spell,
intent is very important: It's
not enough that *you* want
to move on; you have to gra-
ciously allow the other to

move on as well and accept
that this means their feelings
toward you will fully dissipate
at some point. This second
part can be a bit difficult
when you're in the midst of
healing from a broken heart!
If you're struggling with the
thought, you may not be
emotionally ready to cast an
unbinding spell—once it's

cast, you can't take it **back**.
Try meditating or journaling
until you're in the right head-
space; it may take a few days
or even weeks.

What you'll need:

+ Two black candles
* A piece of string
* Scissors or a knife

1. Carve your name on one candle and the name of the person from whom you wish to be unbound on the other.

2. Anoint both candles in peppermint or olive oil, if available, and cleanse them by passing them through the smoke of nag champa or sandalwood incense.

3. Tie the candles together with string, making sure to encircle both at least three times.

4. Light both candles.

5. Repeat the following incantation three times:

No more shall I be bound to [Name], and no more shall [Name] be bound to me.

I sever these ties and
release us both.

I sever my ties
with [Name].

6. When you are finished
   reciting the incantation,
   close with:

So mote it be.

7. Using a knife or scissors, cut
   the string connecting the two.

8. When the candles have fully burnt down, dispose of them separately.

Suggested Enhancements

Nag champa or
sandalwood incense

Peppermint or olive oil
to anoint the candle

Amethyst, aquamarine, or
black tourmaline

PROTECTION SPELL

+ ❋ +

This will keep you safe
from negative energy
and ill intent.

What you'll need:

- ✦ A black candle
- ✳ Salt
- ✳ A small bag or pouch
  (even a Ziploc bag will
  work, if you're in a pinch)
- ✦ Basil
- ✳ Bay leaves
- ✳ Cloves
- ✦ A pen and paper

1. Start by anointing your candle with eucalyptus or rosemary oil, if available, and cleanse it by passing it through the smoke of dragon's blood or sandalwood incense.

2. Make a ring of salt around the candle, large enough to contain both the candle and a small bag or pouch.

3. Next up: Assemble your charm bag. You're going to carry this around with you once the candle has burned down. Start by putting in basil, bay leaves, and cloves—it's up to you how much you want to put in.

4. Then, write the name of whomever you would like

to protect—it's OK if it's just your own name!—and draw a protective circle around it.

5. Fold the paper in half and place it in the charm bag.

6. Place the charm bag directly in front of the candle, inside the ring of salt, and light the candle.

7. Say the following **in**cantation:

*Protect me/us from
those who would
wish me/us harm.*

*Protect me/us from those
who would speak with
malice and ill will.*

*May I/we be safe, secure,
and happy and live a life
filled with peace.*

So mote it be.

8. Once the candle has burned down, dispose of it however you please. Take the charm bag and carry it around with you for protection or leave it in a place where you feel unsafe or at risk—a car, maybe, or perhaps your desk at school or work.

Suggested Enhancements

Dragon's blood or
sandalwood incense

Eucalyptus or rosemary oil
to anoint the candle

Black tourmaline or obsidian
(place these in the pouch)

HEALING SPELL

+ · · ★ · · +

Use this spell to send
healing, compas-
sionate energy to someone
in need. This doesn't have

to necessarily be for physical illness—it can also
be for someone who is
struggling with heartbreak
or loss. (It's also possible
to use this spell to send
healing energy to yourself,
should you need to.)

What you'll need:

+ A white candle
* A photo of the person you wish to heal
* Basil
+ Lavender
* Honey
* A bowl of water
+ White or pink roses

1. Carve the name of the person you wish to heal into the candle; this can

either be along the side of the candle or on top, depending on your preference and how the candle is shaped.

2. Anoint the candle with eucalyptus, lavender, or olive oil, if available, and cleanse it by passing it through the smoke of frankincense and myrrh.

3. Place the photo of the person you'd like to heal in front of the candle.

4. Before the photo, place a bowl of water. Add three drops of honey, as well as basil leaves and lavender.

5. Place the flowers near the candle as an offering.

6. Light the candle, and speak
the following incantation:

*May [Name] grow
strong and healthy.*

*May [Name] know
comfort and compassion.*

*May [Name] experience
the grace of the universe
and heal. So mote it be.*

7. When the candle has completely burned down, pour the water down the sink, and envision pain and suffering going down the drain as well. (If the candle lasts more than one day, pour the water out every morning and refill the bowl. As you refill it, picture yourself pouring out pure, radiant light.)

Suggested
Enhancements

Frankincense and
myrrh incense

Eucalyptus, lavender, or olive
oil *to anoint the candle*

Clear quartz or selenite

This is just a start; with this book, you have all the basic knowledge you'll need to improvise and perform your own spells. Remember: All you need is an intention and a flame, and you can begin manifesting whatever you desire.

The power is in your hands!